DATE DUE			

22235775

599.75   Aylmore, Angela.
AYL

           I like cats

LANE ELEMENTARY SCHOOL
4600 W 123RD ST ALSIP IL 60803

691850 01495   45038A   0002

Things I Like

I Like Cats

Angela Aylmore

Heinemann Library
Chicago, Illinois

© 2007 Heinemann Library
a division of Reed Elsevier Inc.
Chicago, Illinois

Customer Service   888–454–2279
Visit our website at www.heinemannlibrary.com

Photo research by Erica Newbery
Designed by Joanna Hinton-Malivoire
Printed in China by South China Printing Company Limited

11 10 09 08 07
10 9 8 7 6 5 4 3 2 1

Library of Congress Cataloging-in-Publication Data
Aylmore, Angela.
 I like cats / Angela Aylmore.
    p. cm. -- (Things I like)
 Includes bibliographical references and index.
 ISBN-13: 978-1-4034-9270-8 (library binding-hardcover)
 ISBN-10: 1-4034-9270-0 (library binding-hardcover)
 ISBN-13: 978-1-4034-9279-1 (pbk.)
 ISBN-10: 1-4034-9279-4 (pbk.)
 1. Cats--Juvenile literature. I. Title.
 SF445.7.A95 2007
 599.75--dc22

                        2006024840

Acknowledgments
The publishers would like to thank the following for permission to reproduce photographs: Ardea pp. **7** (John Daniels), **9** (John Daniels), **14** (John Daniels); Digital Vision p. **21** (spotted leopard); FLPA p. **21** (black leopard, Jurgen & Christine Sohns); Getty Images pp. **4–5** (all, Photodisc), **10** (Brand X pictures), **11** (Dorling Kindersley), **15** (Photodisc), **16** (The Image Bank), **22** (kitten, Photodisc); Nature Picture Library pp. **17** (Jane Burton), **18** (Anup Shah), **20** (Lucasseck/ARCO); NHPA pp. **19** (Andy Rouse), **22** (lion, Andy Rouse); Photolibrary p. **6** (Dennie & DK. Cody/Workbook, Inc.); Ron Kimball Stock pp. **8** (Ron Kimball), **22** (Himalayan cat, Ron Kimball); Warren Photographic pp. **12–13**.

Cover photograph of a cat reproduced with permission of Alamy/Creatas/Dynamic Graphics Group.

Every effort has been made to contact copyright holders of any material reproduced in this book.
Any omissions will be rectified in subsequent printings if notice is given to the publisher.

Contents

Cats 4

Different Cats.................... 6

Taking Care of My Cat 10

Kittens 14

Wild Cats 18

Do You Like Cats? 22

Glossary.......................... 23

Find Out More................. 24

Index 24

Some words are shown in bold, **like this**. You can find out what they mean by looking in the Glossary.

Cats

I like cats.

I will tell you my favorite
things about cats.

Different Cats

I like the way cats are so different. This Siamese cat has big green eyes.

Bobtail cats have a **stubby** tail.

Himalayan cats have long fur and a cute face.

I like this cat the best. It is a sphynx cat. It has no hair and big ears.

Taking Care of My Cat

I like taking care of my cat.
My cat likes to be **stroked**.

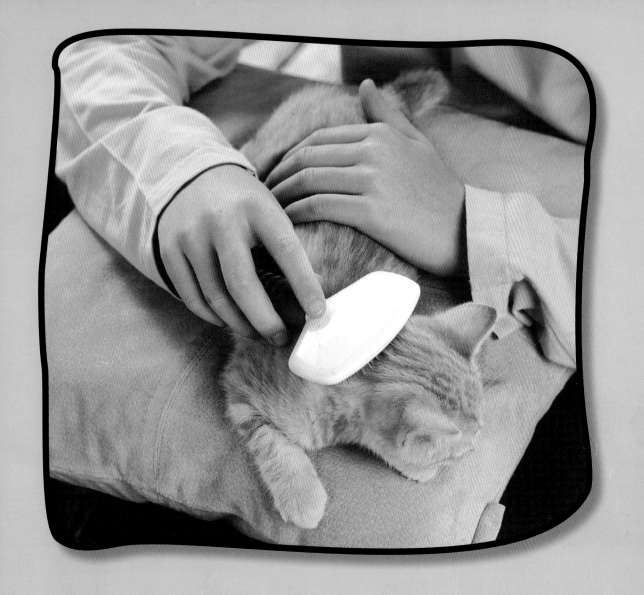

My cat has long fur. I brush
the fur to keep it clean.

I feed my cat twice a day.
I make sure my cat has
water to drink.

13

Kittens

My cat has had **kittens**.
The kittens are very small.

I really like kittens. Kittens have small noses and **whiskers**.

15

Kittens look cute. But kittens have sharp **claws**.

Kittens use their claws
to play with toys.

Wild Cats

A tiger is a big cat. I like tigers. Tigers hide in the grass.

I like lions, too. Male lions have an enormous **mane.**

Cheetahs are very fast.
Cheetahs can run as fast
as a car.

These are both leopards.
Some have spots and some
are all black.

Do You Like Cats?

Now you know why I like cats! Do you like cats, too?

Glossary

claw a hard, sharp nail on a cat's foot

kitten a baby cat

mane long hair on the neck of some
animals, like lions and horses

stroke to move your hand over
something gently

stubby short and thick

whiskers long, stiff hairs that grow
on a cat's face

Find Out More

Gillis, Jennifer Blizin. Cats.
Chicago: Heinemann Library, 2004.

Spilsbury, Richard and Louise Spilsbury.
Watching Lions in Africa. Chicago:
Heinemann Library, 2006.

Find out about big cats at this website:

http://nationalzoo.si.edu/Animals/GreatCats/catskids.cfm

Index

cheetahs 20

claws 16—17

fur 8—9, 11

kittens 14—15, 16—17

leopards 21

lions 19

tigers 18